FROM THE ASHES OF COVID: WE WILL RISE

**Anthology of Covid's effect on
Philadelphia youth and their resilience**

KRISTIN LEWIS

This book is dedicated to those that thought no one was listening. We hear you; we see you, and we respect you.

Message to Youth

Hope Clayton
Program Manager (S125)
Work Ready provided by Urban Affairs Coalition

I am so proud of you for actively participating in the Work Ready program provided by UAC. You started this journey to secure a summer job. You did not know the world would be held hostage by a pandemic. This pandemic altered your lives in an instant. You had to transition from going to school in a building with friends and learning in person to attending school in your home online. Quarantining, masks, and hand sanitizer are your new normal. Guess what? Those things didn't stop you. When your summer job experience morphed into a virtual internship, you did not flinch. Instead, you logged into your online class, determined to excel. You embraced your lessons and, as a result, gained new skills and elevated your confidence. Congratulations on all your accomplishments!

A Word from Coach Kris

CEO and Founder of Breakthrough for Me, LLC

I have always had a passion for educating and empowering those that are underserved. Being able to teach the art of self-publication and plant a seed of creativity for inner- city youth is rewarding. Growing up under strained circumstances in a domestic violence-filled home allowed me to gain empathy and compassion for others in ways far beyond my imagination. The determination and grit I have is because I maintained a solid GPA at a magnet high school while working three jobs because my parents had been laid off.

I hope this book will forever be a symbol to the youth that hard work pays off and that they can accomplish anything they put their minds to and are dedicated to.

The youth participated in a four-week course in which they were compensated for their time spent learning the art of self-publishing. Also, the youth learned about marketing and vending upon publication of this feature.

Breakthrough Team, it is time to market; time to shine, and time to enjoy the fruits of our labor! I believe in each one of you and know you can change the world.

How has COVID-19 affected you?
Jayana Dunlap

COVID-19 has been crazy for me. Not connecting with the outside world is hard. It's been difficult to not be with friends, go outside, or go shopping. Online learning has been challenging because I learn better in person and with a hands-on, classroom approach. Initially, I was scared because I didn't know what was going on. Even though I was scared, I was happy because I didn't have to go to school. That happiness didn't last long because being stuck at home is boring. I want to go to school and learn in person and see my friends.

What did you take away from the 4-week program?

With this program and book, I hope to be able to teach others the skills I've learned. I'm excited to be known as an author and tell my side of the story about how COVID-19 has impacted and my life.

Jayana Dunlap

Jayana Dunlap is from Philadelphia, Pennsylvania, and will be in 11th grade at Belmont Charter High School. Jayana's dream career is to be a maternity nurse and entrepreneur. She enjoys traveling and shopping. A few places she has traveled to include Mexico, Bahamas, and Jamaica. She is the oldest of five. For more information on Jayana Dunlap, please email her at **jayanadunlap@icloud.com**

How has COVID-19 affected you?

Laila Foster-

Stay six feet apart
Only go out if you need to
Contact with others should be rare
If you have symptoms, stay home
Avoid touching your face
Local public health authorities are where
you should get updates
Dispose of personal protection responsibly
Inside most of the time
Safe social activities are a great way to
stay be active
This will soon be behind us
Always wash your hands
Necessary precautions keep everyone safe
Contaminated surfaces should be avoided
Extra time with family is beneficial

Laila Foster

Laila Foster lives in Philadelphia, Pennsylvania and is 14 years old. Laila is in 9th grade at Franklin Learning Center High School and is enrolled in the medical program to help prepare for her future career. Laila wishes to pursue her dreams of becoming a psychologist. She enjoys going shopping, spending time with her friends and family members, and traveling in her free time. Her main goals in life are to be happy, successful, a good leader and role model to others. Laila lives with her parents and younger brother. For more information on Laila Foster, you can email her at **foster.laila@icloud.com**

How has COVID-19 affected you?

Melvin Boulware

The COVID Pandemic has affected daily life. I've missed going to school because I excel with live, in person instruction and not online learning. With online learning, I feel like I'm not only falling behind in my studies, but that I miss socializing with my friends. My stress level is high because I can't go outside as I did before the pandemic. Wearing a mask also adds to my stress, but I know I must wear a mask so I can be safe. I cannot wait for life to go back to a new normal. I look forward to seeing my friends and family and celebrating with them.

Melvin T. Boulware Jr.

Melvin T. Boulware Jr. lives in West Philadelphia, Pennsylvania and is 15 years old. Melvin will be in 11th grade at Belmont Charter High School where his favorite class is math. Melvin plans to study Business management in college so he can be a diesel engineer. He aspires to someday run his family business, a towing, auto body repair, and mechanic company.

Melvin enjoys fast cars, bikes, and loves to travel. So far, he has vacationed to the Dominican Republic, Las Vegas, Washington DC, New York, Canada, and plans to go to Florida for his 16th Birthday. For more information on Melvin Boulware, email him at **hagermanj@rocketmail.com**

How has COVID-19 affected you?

Niyaat Abdus Samad

The pandemic has shown me how life can change and you must adapt. While still trying to complete the rest of this school year, I struggled. We started our final assignments and I underestimated how much time I had left.

The final grades were being released, my grandmother passed away, and my anxiety level was so high. I just didn't know what to do because part of me was saying to just give up, but I knew I had to stay strong. After the looting in our city, we were in lockdown and I began to fear for my safety because I wasn't used to seeing so much violence in my community. The pandemic made me realize that I need to keep my loved ones close because anything could happen. However, I also need to focus on myself and my needs because there isn't going to be a redo of this year. I only get one freshman year.

What did you take away from the 4-week program?

I enjoyed journaling every day while talking about my daily adventures because I am busy, even while quarantining. I've also learned that many people in my city have gone through the same things I have during quarantining. It was also gratifying to be paid for all the work I put into and accomplished during this program.

Niyaat Abdus-Samad

Niyaat Abdus-Samad lives in Philadelphia, Pennsylvania. Niyaat is in 10th grade at Girard She is full of school spirit and is a hard-working, friendly person willing to help others. She is a cheerleader, on the soccer team, and loves to travel. Niyaat dreams of becoming a pediatrician because she enjoys being around people she can help and has a passion for ensuring the health and safety of children. Niyaat lives with her mom, sisters, and brothers. For more information on Niyaat, please email her at **Niyaah0615@gmail.com.**

How has COVID-19 affected me?

Rabiath Abogourin

The COVID-19 pandemic has affected me in many ways; quarantine alone has changed my day-to-day life. I can't go out unless necessary, I must wear a mask when I do go out, and I can't socialize as often as I would normally. Although there are many negative things associated with COVID-19, there have been positive things, too. I got more down time to find my new style and redo my room. There was also a bit less schoolwork and I didn't have to include my SAT scores with college applications. Not having to worry about SAT scores really was positive because even with good, solid scores, it's always causes stress. While COVID-19 has made my academic life easier, it has created challenges for my social and personal life. I miss my friends and going out, but COVID-19 has also allowed me to reflect and explore other interests. I've become interested in drawing, learned to sew, and have improved my writing skills. One of the most positive things is that I've been able to spend so much more time with my family.

What do you hope to accomplish by participating in the Self-Publishing cohort?

I hope to give future students the motivation to continue to work hard and be optimistic through all hard times. I believe that there is always a bright side to every situation, so I want to be able to help others see that brighter side!

Rabiath Abogourin

Rabiath Abogourin lives in Philadelphia, Pennsylvania and will be in 12th grade at Commonwealth Charter Academy. Throughout high school, Rabiath has volunteered at a local hospital and a homeless shelter. She has been involved with many programs and has spent countless hours working with Special Education and Autistic children. Rabiath is a member of the National Honor Society and will be one of the Officers as a Parliamentarian in the upcoming school year. She strives to do her best and give 100 percent in all she does.

Rabiath dreams of becoming a researcher, scientist, or doctor. She loves these fields because she wants to help others and give back to her community and the world. For more information on Rabiath Abogourin, please email her at **rabogourin2021@gmail.com**

How has COVID-19 affected me?

Sanaa Fowler

COVID-19 has affected me in so many ways, good and bad. Originally when my school announced that we wouldn't have school for two weeks, I was excited. However, that two weeks would soon turn into a life-changing six months. COVID-19 has taught me how to adapt to situations and to move efficiently. However, it was draining and tough, especially with school. My daily online school schedule was different, and I struggled to learn online, as I'm a hands on, in person learner.

In addition to academic challenges, COVID-19 presented day to day social challenges. Everything was closed, a curfew was put in place, and I was forced to stay inside. However, on the positive side, being stuck inside allowed me to take time to focus on myself and my goals. I was able to hone some of my cosmetology skills.

During quarantine, I realized the importance of family and friends and really caring about those you love the most. It was scary as worldwide COVID-19 cases rose, daily. I worried about my friends and family, especially my grandma, who was more susceptible due to her age. My mom is an essential worker, she was in danger every shift. Though COVID-19 was scary, it still taught me to overcome obstacles and adapt to new situations.

What do you hope to accomplish by participating in the Self-Publishing cohort?

I hope that by being part of this I will be able to attract a sponsor for college as well as information and opportunities for college scholarships. There are going to be so many paths, possibilities, and accomplishments for my future. I hope to take advantage of all of them.

Sanaa Fowler

Sanaa Fowler lives in Philadelphia, Pennsylvania and is going to be in 10th grade at Mercy Career & Technical High School. Sanaa is hardworking, independent, loving, and caring. She loves to learn new things as well as teach others new things. In her free time, Sanaa enjoys reading and spending time with her family and friends. She hopes to inspire the children in her life to work hard for something they want to accomplish. Sanaa's future goal is to be a cosmetologist. She is focused on this goal and will not let anything stand in the way of her success. For more information on Sanaa Fowler, please email her at

fowlersanaa4@gmail.com

How has COVID-19 affected me?

Assata Johnson-

I've been fortunate that COVID-19 hasn't impacted me or anyone in my life, directly. However, it did affect my academics. My school closed in March and while it seemed relatively minor for the first month, once virtual learning began, I struggled because I am a hands-on and visual learner. Staying in one place and on a computer for hours was challenging for me. I was able to get a laptop, so that was helpful and as I got used to learning online, I was able to become a better auditory learner.

This summer, I was supposed to take part in a five week mandatory summer bridge program at The Community College of Philadelphia before attending Parkway Center City Middle College. However, this program was cancelled because of COVID-19. It's now a one week virtual mandatory workshop.

I also had plans to travel overseas, like I've done every year since fifth grade, but COVID-19 has cancelled those plans, too.

Daily, I like to stay close to home and be with my family, so wearing a mask is not a big issue for me. I'm lucky to be able to stay at home and focus on my studies and my future.

What did you take away from the 4-week program?

I was surprised by the feeling of enjoying something I never thought I would. Being part of something so positive and welcoming was an empowering feeling. It was great to gain new interests and invest time in something that I begrudgingly started, but learned to love.

Assata Johnson

Assata Johnson, named after social activist and former member of the Black Liberation Army, Assata Shakur, lives in Philadelphia, Pennsylvania and is 14 years old. Assata is a recent graduate of Amy Northwest Middle School and will be in 9th grade at Parkway Center City Middle College. Assata is very independent, determined, self- disciplined, and motivated. Assata's favorite subjects in school are Math and English. She was the president of the Junior Honor Society and participated in the Art Museum program, Project L.O.V.E., and Youth Court. She also was captain of the volleyball team and the catcher for the softball team.

Though Assata is just beginning high school, she is thinking about and planning for her future. After high school, Assata plans to join United States Marine Corps and become an active duty Marine. While in the Marine Corps, Assata's goal is to attend college to study law and criminal justice.

Assata enjoys traveling, drawing, writing, playing sports, and learning about topics that school does not teach. Some places she has traveled include Mexico, Dominican Republic, Dubai, and Abu Dhabi.

The summer before COVID-19, Assata attended the Pennsylvania State Police Troop K Camp Cadet Program. While at camp, she was taught self-discipline and gained a better understanding of law enforcement. She was also taught about firearm safety, archery, forensic science, etc. Assata was challenged mentally, physically, and emotionally. On graduation day, Assata received the 2019 Female Honor Cadet award and was invited to the 2020 Commissioner's Honor Camp.

Assata's goals in life are to be healthy, happy, and successful. She knows what she wants out of life and how to get it. Her motto is, "Work hard for what you want!" For more information on Assata Johnson, please email her at **Mlga05@yahoo.com**

About Coach Kris

Kristin Lewis Fullenwellen was born and raised in Philadelphia, Pennsylvania. Kristin is an author, wife, and mother of two. She is an entrepreneur with great passion for assisting the youth and their families because during her childhood she lived a life that was strained and filled with domestic abuse.

Kristin obtained a Bachelor of Arts in Psychology from Temple University. She has written two children's books, *You are Special*, that promotes self-love and respect for others, and *What Comes on the Page before Me?* that promotes early literacy and is a favorite bedtime story for preschoolers.

For more information on Kristin, visit her at Instagram @Kristhechosen1, like her Facebook fan page at **www.facebook.com/authorklewis,** or visit her website at **www.Breakthroughforme.com** and start your journey to self-publishing today.

TEAM

S
P
O
N
S
O
R
S

Urban Affairs Coalition
@uacoalition/@uacYouthemployment
www.uac.org

Focus Youth Network
@FOCUSYOUTHNETWORK
www.FocusYouthnetwork.org

Ambitious Images Photography
@Ambitiousimagesphotography

S P O N S O R S

Shirts4Believers
www.Shirts4Believers.com

God Over Everything Apparel
@GOEApparelCo
www.GodOverEverythingApparel.com